COOKING FOR TODAY

Pasta

p

chicken & pasta broth

serves six

12 oz/350 g boneless
   chicken breasts

2 tbsp corn oil

1 medium onion, diced

1½ cups carrots, diced

9 oz/250 g cauliflower flowerets

3¾ cups chicken bouillon

2 tsp dried mixed herbs

1¼ cups small pasta shapes

salt and pepper

freshly grated Parmesan
   cheese, optional

VARIATION

Broccoli flowerets can be used to replace the cauliflower flowerets. Substitute 2 tbsp of chopped fresh mixed herbs for the dried mixed herbs, if you wish.

---

1 Finely dice the chicken breasts with a sharp knife. Remove and discard any skin.

2 Heat the oil in a large heavy-bottomed pan or skillet over a medium-high heat. Add the diced chicken and the vegetables and quickly cook until they are lightly colored.

3 Stir in the bouillon and herbs. Bring to a boil and add the pasta shapes. Return to a boil, cover, and simmer for 10 minutes, stirring occasionally to prevent the pasta shapes sticking together.

4 Season to taste with salt and pepper, sprinkle with Parmesan cheese (if using) and serve.

tomato & pasta soup

serves four

4 tbsp unsalted butter

1 large onion, chopped

2½ cups vegetable bouillon

2 lb/900 g Italian plum tomatoes,
    peeled and chopped coarsely

pinch of baking soda

2 cups dried fusilli

1 tbsp superfine sugar

⅝ cup heavy cream

salt and pepper

fresh basil leaves, to garnish

1 Melt the butter in a large pan over a medium heat. Add the onion and cook for 3 minutes. Add 1¼ cups of vegetable bouillon to the pan, with the tomatoes, and baking soda. Bring to a boil, then reduce the heat and simmer for 20 minutes.

2 Remove the pan from the heat and let cool. Transfer the soup to a blender and process until smooth. Pour through a fine strainer back into the rinsed out pan.

3 Add the remaining vegetable bouillon and the pasta, and season to taste with salt and pepper.

4 Add the sugar to the pan and bring to a boil over a medium heat, then reduce the heat and simmer for about 15 minutes.

5 Ladle the soup into a warmed tureen, swirl the cream on top of the soup and garnish with fresh basil leaves. Serve immediately.

minestrone soup

serves eight–ten

3 garlic cloves

3 large onions

2 celery stalks

2 large carrots

2 large potatoes

¾ cup green beans

3½ oz/100 g zucchini

4 tbsp butter

¼ cup olive oil

2 oz/55 g rindless fatty bacon,
    diced finely

6⅛ cups vegetable or
    chicken bouillon

1 bunch fresh basil, chopped finely

⅜ cup chopped tomatoes

2 tbsp tomato paste

3½ oz/100 g fresh Parmesan
    cheese peel

¼ cup dried spaghetti, broken up

salt and pepper

freshly grated Parmesan cheese,
    to serve

1 Finely chop the garlic, onions, celery stalks, carrots, potatoes, beans, and zucchini with a sharp knife.

2 Heat the butter and oil together in a large pan over a medium heat. Add the bacon and cook for 2 minutes. Add the garlic and onion, and cook for 2 minutes. Stir in the celery, carrots, and potatoes and cook for 2 minutes.

3 Add the chopped beans to the pan and cook for 2 minutes. Stir in the zucchini and cook for an additional 2 minutes. Cover the pan and cook all the vegetables, stirring frequently, for 15 minutes.

4 Add the bouillon, basil, tomatoes, tomato paste, and cheese peel and season to taste. Bring to a boil, then reduce the heat and simmer for 1 hour. Remove the cheese peel and discard.

5 Add the pasta to the pan and cook for 20 minutes.

6 Ladle the soup into warmed soup bowls, sprinkle with freshly grated Parmesan cheese and serve.

COOK'S TIP

There are almost as many recipes for minestrone as there are cooks in Italy! You can add almost any vegetables you like and canned beans, such as lima beans.

chicken ravioli in tarragon broth

serves six

8 cups chicken bouillon

2 tbsp finely chopped fresh
tarragon leaves

freshly grated Parmesan cheese,
to serve

HOMEMADE PASTA DOUGH

1 cup pasta or white bread flour,
plus extra if needed

2 tbsp fresh tarragon leaves, with
stems removed

1 egg

1 egg, separated

1 tsp extra virgin olive oil

2–3 tbsp water

FILLING

7 oz/200 g cooked chicken,
chopped coarsely

½ tsp grated lemon peel

2 tbsp chopped mixed fresh
tarragon, chives, and parsley

4 tbsp whipping cream

a pinch of salt and pepper

1 To make the pasta, mix the flour, tarragon, and salt into a food processor and mix together. Beat the egg, egg yolk, oil, and 2 tablespoons of the water together. With the machine still running, pour in the egg mixture and process until it forms a ball, leaving the sides of the bowl virtually clean. If the dough is crumbly, add the remaining water. If the dough is sticky, add 1–2 tablespoons of flour and continue kneading in the food processor until a ball forms. Wrap and chill in the refrigerator for 30 minutes. Set aside the egg white.

2 To make the filling, put the chicken, lemon peel, and mixed herbs into a food processor and season to taste with salt and pepper. Chop finely, by pulsing. Scrape into a bowl and stir in the cream. Taste and adjust the seasoning, if necessary.

3 Divide the pasta dough in half. Cover one half with a damp dish towel and roll the other half on a floured counter as thinly as possible, less than 1/16 inch/1.5 mm. Cut out rectangles 4 x 2 inches/10 x 5 cm.

4 Put rounded teaspoons of filling on one half of the dough pieces. Brush around the edges with the egg white and fold in half. Press the edges gently but firmly to seal. Arrange the ravioli in one layer on a cookie sheet, dusted generously with flour. Repeat with remaining dough. Let the ravioli dry in a cool place for 15 minutes, or chill in the refrigerator for 1–2 hours.

5 Bring a large pan of lightly salted water to a boil over a medium heat. Drop in half the ravioli and cook for 4–6 minutes, or until done. Drain the ravioli on a clean dish cloth while cooking the remainder.

6 Meanwhile, put the bouillon and tarragon in a large pan, then bring to a boil over a medium heat. Reduce the heat to bubble very gently. Cover and simmer for 15 minutes, to infuse. Add the cooked ravioli to the bouillon and simmer for 5 minutes until heated through. Ladle into 6 large, warmed soup bowls and serve immediately with Parmesan cheese.

vermicelli & vegetable soup

serves four

1 small eggplant

2 large tomatoes

1 potato, peeled

1 carrot, peeled

1 leek

14½ oz/420 g canned
cannellini beans

3¾ cups hot vegetable or
chicken bouillon

2 tsp dried basil

½ oz/15 g dried porcini mushrooms,
soaked for 20 minutes in enough
almost boiling water to cover

¼ cup dried vermicelli

3 tbsp Pesto (see page 9)

freshly grated Parmesan cheese, to
serve (optional)

1 Slice the eggplant into rings,
about ½-inch/1-cm thick, then cut
each ring into 4 pieces.

2 Cut the tomatoes and potato into
small dice. Cut the carrot into
sticks, about 1-inch/2.5-cm long and
cut the leek into rings.

3 Put the beans and their liquid in a
pan. Add the eggplant, tomatoes,
potato, carrot, and leek, then stir.

4 Add the bouillon to the pan and
bring to a boil over a medium
heat. Reduce the heat and simmer for
15 minutes.

5 Add the basil, dried mushrooms,
their soaking liquid, and the
vermicelli and cook for 5 minutes.

6 Remove the pan from the heat and
stir in the Pesto (see page 9).

7 Ladle the soup into 4 large,
warmed soup bowls and serve
with Parmesan cheese (if using).

potato & parsley soup with pesto

serves four

3 slices rindless, smoked
   fatty bacon

1 lb/450 g mealy potatoes

1 lb/450 g onions

2 tbsp butter

2½ cups chicken bouillon

2½ cups milk

¾ cup dried conchigliette

⅝ cup heavy cream

1 tbsp chopped fresh parsley

salt and pepper

PESTO SAUCE

1 cup finely chopped fresh parsley

2 garlic cloves, minced

⅔ cup pine nuts, minced

2 tbsp chopped fresh basil leaves

⅔ cup freshly grated
   Parmesan cheese

white pepper

⅝ cup olive oil

TO SERVE

freshly grated Parmesan cheese

garlic bread

1 To make the pesto sauce, put all the ingredients into a blender or food processor and process for 2 minutes, or blend by hand.

2 Chop the bacon, potatoes, and onions. Put the bacon into a pan and cook over a medium heat for 4 minutes. Add the butter, potatoes, and onions and cook for 12 minutes.

3 Add the bouillon and milk to the pan, then bring to a boil and cook for 10 minutes. Add the pasta and cook for 12–14 minutes.

4 Blend in the cream and simmer for 5 minutes. Add the parsley and 2 tablespoons of pesto sauce. Ladle the soup into bowls and serve with the remaining pesto sauce, Parmesan cheese, and garlic bread.

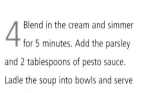

italian fish stew

serves four

2 tbsp olive oil

2 red onions, chopped finely

1 garlic clove, minced

2 zucchini, sliced

14 oz/400 g canned
   chopped tomatoes

3¾ cups fish or vegetable bouillon

¾ cup small dried pasta shapes

12 oz/350 g firm white fish, such
   as cod, haddock, or hake

1 tbsp chopped fresh basil or
   oregano or 1 tsp dried oregano

1 tsp finely grated lemon peel

1 tbsp cornstarch

1 tbsp water

salt and pepper

4 fresh basil or oregano sprigs,
   to garnish

1 Heat the oil in a large pan over a low heat. Add the onions and garlic and cook, stirring occasionally, for about 5 minutes, or until softened. Add the zucchini and cook, stirring frequently, for 2–3 minutes.

2 Add the tomatoes and bouillon to the pan and bring to a boil over a medium heat. Add the pasta, bring back to a boil, then reduce the heat, cover and simmer for 5 minutes.

3 Skin and bone the fish, then cut it into chunks. Add to the pan with the basil or oregano and lemon peel and simmer gently for 5 minutes, or until the fish is opaque and flakes easily (take care not to overcook it) and the pasta is done.

4 Blend the cornstarch with the water to form a smooth paste and stir into the stew. Cook for 2 minutes,

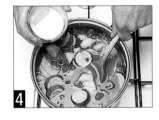

stirring constantly, until thickened. Season to taste with salt and pepper.

5 Ladle the stew into 4 large, warmed soup bowls. Garnish with fresh basil or oregano sprigs and serve immediately.

chicken & bean soup

serves four

2 tbsp butter

3 scallions, chopped

2 garlic cloves, minced

1 fresh marjoram sprig, chopped finely

12 oz/350 g boned chicken
    breasts, diced

5 cups chicken bouillon

12 oz/350 g canned garbanzo
    beans, drained

1 bouquet garni sachet

1 red bell pepper, diced

1 green bell pepper, diced

1 cup small dried pasta shapes,
    such as elbow macaroni

salt and white pepper

croutons, to serve

1 Melt the butter in a large pan over a medium heat. Add the scallions, garlic, marjoram, and diced chicken and cook, stirring frequently, for 5 minutes.

2 Add the chicken bouillon, garbanzo beans, and bouquet garni sachet, then season to taste with salt and white pepper.

3 Bring the soup to a boil over a medium heat, then reduce the heat and simmer for about 2 hours.

4 Add the diced bell peppers and pasta shapes to the pan, then simmer for an additional 20 minutes.

5 Ladle the soup into 4 warmed soup bowls and garnish with croutons. Serve immediately.

11

ravioli alla parmigiana

serves four

285 g/10 oz Homemade Pasta
   Dough (see page 6), made
   without fresh tarragon
5 cups veal bouillon
1 egg white, beaten
freshly grated Parmesan cheese,
   to serve
FILLING
1 cup freshly grated
   Parmesan cheese
1⅔ cup fine white bread crumbs
2 eggs
½ cup Espagnole Sauce
   (see Cook's Tip)
1 small onion, chopped finely
1 tsp freshly grated nutmeg

1 Make the Homemade Pasta
Dough (see page 6). Carefully roll
out 2 sheets of the pasta dough on a
lightly floured counter and cover with a
damp dish towel while you make the
filling for the ravioli.

2 To make the ravioli filling, mix the
Parmesan cheese, bread crumbs,
eggs, Espagnole Sauce (see Cook's
Tip), onion, and the freshly grated
nutmeg together in a large bowl.

3 Put spoonfuls of the filling at
regular intervals on 1 sheet of the
pasta dough. Cover with the second
sheet of dough, then cut into squares
and seal the edges with egg white.

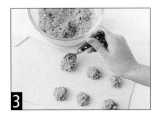

4 Bring the veal bouillon to a boil in
a large pan over a medium heat.
Add the ravioli and cook for about
15 minutes, or until cooked through.

5 Transfer the ravioli to 4 large,
warmed serving bowls, sprinkle
generously with Parmesan cheese and
serve immediately.

COOK'S TIP

For Espagnole Sauce, melt 2 tbsp
butter and stir in ¼ cup all-
purpose flour. Cook over a low
heat, stirring, until lightly
colored. Add 1 tsp tomato paste,
then stir in scant 2 cups hot veal
bouillon, 1 tbsp Madeira and
1½ tsp white wine vinegar. Dice
1 oz/25 g each bacon, carrot, and
onion and ½ oz/15 g each celery,
leek, and fennel. Cook with a
fresh thyme sprig and a bay leaf
in oil until soft. Drain, add to the
sauce and simmer for 2–3 hours.
Strain before using.

spaghetti olio e aglio

serves four

½ cup olive oil

3 garlic cloves, minced

1 lb/450 g fresh spaghetti

3 tbsp coarsely chopped
   fresh parsley

salt and pepper

1 Heat the oil in a medium-size heavy-bottomed pan over a low heat. Add the garlic and a pinch of salt and cook, stirring constantly, until golden brown, then remove the pan from the heat. Do not let the garlic burn as it will taint the flavor of the oil. (If it does burn, you will have to start all over again!)

2 Meanwhile, bring a large pan of lightly salted water to a boil over a medium heat. Add the pasta and cook for about 2–3 minutes, or until done. Drain the pasta thoroughly and return to the pan.

3 Add the oil and garlic mixture to the pasta and toss to coat thoroughly. Season with pepper to taste, add the chopped fresh parsley and toss to coat again.

4 Transfer the pasta to a large, warmed serving dish and serve.

creamed veal kidneys with pesto sauce

serves four

5 tbsp butter

12 veal kidneys, trimmed and
    sliced thinly

1½ cups white mushrooms, sliced

1 tsp English mustard

pinch of freshly grated gingerroot

2 tbsp dry sherry

⅝ cup heavy cream

2 tbsp Pesto Sauce (see page 9)

3½ cups dried penne

4 slices of hot toast cut
    into triangles

salt and pepper

4 fresh parsley sprigs, to garnish

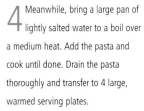

1 Melt the butter in a large skillet over a low heat. Add the kidneys and cook for 4 minutes. Transfer to an ovenproof dish and keep warm.

2 Add the mushrooms to the skillet, and cook for about 2 minutes.

3 Add the mustard and ginger to the skillet. Season to taste with salt and pepper. Cook for 2 minutes, then add the sherry, cream, and Pesto Sauce (see page 9). Cook for an additional 3 minutes, then pour the sauce over the kidneys. Cook in a preheated oven at 375°F/190°C, for about 10 minutes.

4 Meanwhile, bring a large pan of lightly salted water to a boil over a medium heat. Add the pasta and cook until done. Drain the pasta thoroughly and transfer to 4 large, warmed serving plates.

5 Put the kidneys in the sauce on top of the pasta. Put a few triangles of hot toast around the kidneys, garnish with fresh parsley sprigs and serve immediately.

chorizo & exotic mushrooms

serves six

1 lb 7 oz/650 g dried vermicelli

⅓ cup olive oil

2 garlic cloves, chopped finely

4½ oz/125 g chorizo, sliced

8 oz/225 g exotic mushrooms

3 fresh red chilies, chopped

2 tbsp freshly grated
  Parmesan cheese

salt and pepper

10 anchovy fillets, to garnish

COOK'S TIP

Always obtain exotic mushrooms from a reliable source and never pick them yourself unless you are absolutely certain of their identity. If you can't find exotic mushrooms, use portobello or crimini mushrooms or a mixture of the two instead.

1 Bring a large pan of lightly salted water to a boil over a medium heat. Add the pasta and cook until just done. Drain the pasta thoroughly, put onto a large, warmed serving plate, and keep warm.

2 Meanwhile, heat the oil in a large skillet over a low heat. Add the garlic and cook for 1 minute. Add the chorizo and exotic mushrooms and cook for 4 minutes, then add the red chilies and cook for 1 minute, or until the mushrooms are cooked through.

3 Pour the chorizo and exotic mushroom mixture over the pasta and season to taste with salt and pepper. Transfer to 4 warmed serving plates, sprinkle over the Parmesan cheese and garnish with a lattice of anchovy fillets. Serve immediately.

olive, bell pepper & cherry tomato pasta

serves four

2 cups dried orecchiette

2 tbsp olive oil

2 tbsp butter

2 garlic cloves, minced

1 green bell pepper, sliced thinly

1 yellow bell pepper, sliced thinly

16 cherry tomatoes, halved

1 tbsp chopped oregano

½ cup dry white wine

2 tbsp pitted ripe black olives, cut
  into fourths

1½ cups arugula

salt and pepper

TO GARNISH

freshly grated Parmesan cheese

1 fresh oregano sprig

COOK'S TIP

Ensure that the pan is large
enough to prevent the pasta
from sticking together
during cooking.

1 Bring a large pan of lightly salted water to a boil over a medium heat. Add the pasta and cook for 8–10 minutes, or until done. Drain.

2 Heat the oil and butter in a pan over a low heat. Add the garlic and cook for 30 seconds. Add the bell peppers and cook, stirring constantly, for 3–4 minutes.

3 Stir in the cherry tomatoes, oregano, wine, and olives, and cook for 3–4 minutes. Season to taste with salt and pepper and stir in the arugula until just wilted.

4 Transfer the pasta to a warmed serving dish, spoon the sauce over and mix. Garnish with Parmesan cheese and an oregano sprig. Serve.

spaghetti alla carbonara

serves four

15 oz/425 g dried spaghetti

1 tbsp olive oil

1 large onion, sliced thinly

2 garlic cloves, chopped

6 oz/175 g rindless bacon, cut into
thin strips

2 tbsp butter

1½ cups mushrooms, sliced thinly

1¼ cups heavy cream

3 eggs, beaten

1 cup freshly grated Parmesan
cheese, plus extra to
serve (optional)

salt and pepper

fresh sage sprigs, to garnish

COOK'S TIP

The key to success with this
recipe is not to overcook the
egg. That is why it is important
to keep all the ingredients
hot enough just to cook the
egg—work rapidly to avoid
scrambling it.

1 Bring a large pan of lightly salted water to a boil over a medium heat. Add the pasta and cook for about 8–10 minutes, or until done. Drain the pasta thoroughly, return to the pan, and keep warm.

2 Meanwhile, heat the remaining oil in a skillet over a medium heat. Add the onion and cook until translucent. Add the garlic and bacon and cook until the bacon is crisp. Transfer to a warmed plate.

3 Melt the butter in the skillet over a low heat. Add the mushrooms and cook for 3–4 minutes. Return the bacon mixture to the skillet. Cover and keep warm.

4 Mix the cream, eggs, and cheese together in a large bowl, then season to taste with salt and pepper.

5 Working very quickly, tip the pasta into the bacon and mushroom mixture and pour over the eggs. Using 2 forks, toss the pasta quickly into the egg and cream mixture. Garnish with sage sprigs and serve immediately with extra Parmesan cheese, if you wish.

tricolor timballini

serves four

1 tbsp butter, softened

1 cup dry white bread crumbs

6 oz/175 g dried tricolor spaghetti,
   broken into 2-inch/5-cm lengths

2 tbsp olive oil

1 egg yolk

1 cup freshly grated Swiss cheese

1¼ cups Béchamel Sauce
   (see page 44)

1 onion, chopped finely

1 bay leaf

⅔ cup dry white wine

⅔ cup strained tomatoes

1 tbsp tomato paste

salt and pepper

1 Lightly oil 4 ¾-cup molds or ramekins with the butter. Evenly coat the insides with half the bread crumbs.

2 Bring a pan of lightly salted water to a boil over a medium heat. Add the pasta and cook for about 8–10 minutes, or until done. Drain the pasta thoroughly and transfer to a mixing bowl. Add the egg yolk and cheese to the pasta and season to taste with salt and pepper.

3 Stir the Béchamel Sauce (see page 44) into the pasta and mix well. Spoon the pasta mixture into the prepared molds and sprinkle the remaining bread crumbs over the top.

4 Stand the molds on a cookie sheet and cook in a preheated oven at 425°F/220°C, for 20 minutes. Remove the cookie sheet from the oven and set the molds aside for 10 minutes.

5 To make the sauce, heat the oil in a pan over a low heat. Add the onion and bay leaf and cook for 2–3 minutes. Stir in the wine, strained tomatoes, and tomato paste and season to taste with salt and pepper. Simmer for 20 minutes until thickened. Remove the bay leaf and discard.

6 Turn the timballini out onto 4 large, warmed serving plates and serve immediately with the tomato sauce.

pasta omelet

serves two

4 tbsp olive oil

1 small onion, chopped

1 fennel bulb, sliced thinly

4 oz/115 g potato, diced

1 garlic clove, chopped

4 eggs

1 tbsp chopped fresh Italian parsley

pinch of chili powder

2¼ cups cooked short pasta

2 tbsp stuffed green olives, halved

salt and pepper

fresh marjoram sprigs, to garnish

tomato salad, to serve

1 Heat half the oil in a heavy skillet over a low heat. Add the onion, fennel, and potato and cook, stirring occasionally, for 8–10 minutes, or until the potato is just tender.

2 Stir in the garlic and cook for 1 minute. Remove the skillet from the heat, transfer the vegetables to a plate and set aside.

3 Beat the eggs until frothy. Stir in the parsley and season with salt, pepper, and a pinch of chili powder.

4 Heat 1 tablespoon of the remaining oil in a clean skillet. Add half the egg mixture to the skillet, then add the cooked vegetables, pasta, and half the olives. Pour in the remaining egg mixture and cook until the sides start to set.

5 Lift up the edges of the omelet with a spatula to let the uncooked egg to spread underneath. Cook until the underside is light golden brown.

6 Slide the omelet out of the skillet onto a plate. Wipe the pan with paper towels and heat the remaining oil. Invert the omelet into the pan and cook until the other side is golden.

7 Slide the omelet onto a large, warmed serving dish and garnish with the remaining olives and marjoram sprigs. Cut into wedges and serve with a tomato salad.

spaghetti with ricotta cheese sauce

serves four

12 oz/350 g dried spaghetti

3 tbsp butter

2 tbsp chopped fresh Italian parsley

salt and pepper

fresh Italian parsley sprigs,
   to garnish

SAUCE

1 cup freshly ground almonds

½ cup ricotta cheese

pinch of freshly grated nutmeg

pinch of ground cinnamon

⅔ cup sour cream

2 tbsp olive oil

½ cup hot chicken bouillon

1 tbsp pine nuts

COOK'S TIP

Use 2 large forks to toss spaghetti or other long pasta, so that it is thoroughly coated with the sauce. Special spaghetti forks are available from some cookware departments and large kitchen stores.

1 Bring a pan of lightly salted water to a boil over a medium heat. Add the pasta and cook for about 8–10 minutes, or until done.

2 Drain the pasta thoroughly, then return to the pan and toss the pasta with the butter and chopped parsley. Set the pan aside, cover, and keep warm.

3 To make the sauce, mix the ground almonds, ricotta cheese, nutmeg, cinnamon, and sour cream together in a small pan and stir over low heat to a thick paste. Gradually stir in the oil. When the oil has been fully incorporated, gradually stir in the hot chicken bouillon, until smooth. Season with pepper to taste.

4 Transfer the pasta to a large, warmed serving dish, pour the sauce over it, and toss together well with 2 forks (see Cook's Tip). Sprinkle over the pine nuts, garnish with the sprigs of fresh Italian parsley, and serve immediately.

tagliatelle with garlic butter

serves four

3 cups white bread flour, plus extra
  for dredging

2 tsp salt

4 eggs, beaten

2 tbsp olive oil

5 tbsp butter, melted

3 garlic cloves, chopped finely

2 tbsp chopped fresh parsley

pepper

1 Sift the flour into a large bowl and stir in the salt.

2 Make a well in the center of the dry ingredients and add the eggs and the oil. Using a wooden spoon, stir in the eggs, gradually drawing in the flour. After a few minutes the dough will be too stiff to use a spoon and you will need to use your fingers.

3 Once all of the flour has been incorporated, turn the dough out onto a lightly floured counter and knead for about 5 minutes, or until smooth and elastic. If you find the dough is too wet, add a little more flour and continue kneading. Cover with plastic wrap and chill in the refrigerator for about 30 minutes. This makes the dough easier to roll and less likely to tear.

4 Roll out the pasta dough thinly and create the pasta shapes required. This can be done by hand or using a pasta machine. Results from a machine are usually neater and thinner, but not necessarily better.

5 To make the tagliatelle by hand, fold the thinly rolled pasta sheets into 3 and cut out long, thin strips, about ½-inch/1-cm wide.

6 Bring a large pan of water to a boil over a medium heat. Add the pasta and cook for 2–3 minutes, or until done. The texture should have a slight bite to it. Drain and return the pasta to the pan.

7 Mix the butter, garlic, and parsley together in a small bowl. Stir into the pasta, season with a little pepper to taste, and serve immediately.

tagliarini with gorgonzola

serves four

2 tbsp butter

8 oz/225 g Gorgonzola cheese, crumbled coarsely

⅝ cup heavy cream

2 tbsp dry white wine

1 tsp cornstarch

4 fresh sage sprigs, chopped finely

14 oz/400 g dried tagliarini

2 tbsp olive oil

salt and white pepper

1 fresh sage sprig, to garnish

1 Melt the butter in a heavy-bottomed pan over a low heat. Stir in 6 oz/175 g of the Gorgonzola cheese and melt for about 2 minutes.

2 Add the cream, wine, and cornstarch and beat with a wooden spoon until blended.

3 Stir in the sage and season to taste with salt and white pepper. Bring to a boil over a low heat, beating constantly, until the sauce thickens. Remove from the heat and set aside while you cook the pasta.

4 Bring a large pan of lightly salted water to a boil over a medium heat. Add the pasta and cook for 12–14 minutes, or until done. Drain the pasta thoroughly, and toss in the oil. Transfer the pasta to a warmed serving dish and keep warm.

5 Return the pan containing the sauce to a low heat and warm through, beating constantly. Spoon the Gorgonzola sauce over the pasta. Garnish with a fresh sage sprig and sprinkle over the remaining cheese. Serve immediately.

COOK'S TIP

Gorgonzola is one of the world's oldest veined cheeses. When buying, check that it is creamy yellow with green veining. Avoid hard or discolored cheese. It should have a rich, piquant aroma, not a bitter smell.

spaghetti with smoked salmon

serves four

1 lb/450 g dried spaghetti

1 tbsp olive oil

1 cup heavy cream

⅔ cup whiskey or brandy

4½ oz/125 g smoked salmon

pinch of cayenne pepper

2 tbsp chopped fresh cilantro
 or parsley

¾ cup crumbled feta cheese
 (drained weight)

pepper

fresh cilantro or parsley sprigs,
 to garnish

COOK'S TIP

Serve this rich and luxurious dish
with salad greens tossed in a
lemony dressing.

1 Bring a large pan of lightly salted water to a boil over a medium heat. Add the pasta and cook until done. Drain the pasta thoroughly, return to the pan and sprinkle over the oil. Cover, shake the pan, set aside, and keep warm.

2 Pour the cream into a small pan and bring to simmering point, but do not let it boil. Pour the whiskey or brandy into another small pan and bring to simmering point, but do not let it boil. Remove both pans from the heat and mix the cream and whiskey or brandy together.

3 Cut the smoked salmon into thin strips and add to the cream mixture. Season to taste with cayenne and pepper. Just before serving, stir in the chopped fresh cilantro or parsley.

4 Transfer the pasta to a warmed serving dish, pour over the sauce and toss thoroughly with 2 large forks. Transfer to 4 warmed plates, sprinkle over the feta cheese and garnish with the cilantro sprigs. Serve immediately.

spicy tomato tagliatelle

serves four

3 tbsp butter

1 onion, chopped finely

1 garlic clove, minced

2 small fresh red chilies, seeded
and diced

1 lb/450 g tomatoes, peeled,
seeded, and diced

¾ cup vegetable bouillon

2 tbsp tomato paste

1 tsp sugar

1 lb 7 oz/650 g fresh green
and white tagliatelle or
12 oz/350 g dried tagliatelle

salt and pepper

1 Melt the butter in a large pan over a medium-low heat. Add the onion and garlic and cook for about 3–4 minutes, or until softened.

2 Add the chilies to the pan and continue cooking for about 2 minutes.

3 Add the tomatoes and bouillon, then reduce the heat and simmer for 10 minutes, stirring.

4 Pour the sauce into a food processor and blend for 1 minute, or until smooth. Alternatively, push the sauce through a strainer.

5 Return the sauce to the pan and add the tomato paste, sugar, and salt and pepper to taste. Gently heat over a low heat, until piping hot.

6 Bring a large pan of lightly salted water to a boil over a medium heat. Add the pasta and cook until done. Drain the pasta thoroughly. Transfer to 4 warmed serving plates and serve tossed in the tomato sauce.

pasta with cheese & broccoli

serves four

10½ oz/300 g dried tagliatelle
  tricolore (plain, spinach- and
  tomato-flavored noodles)
2½ cups broccoli, broken into
  small flowerets
1½ cups mascarpone cheese
1 cup blue cheese, chopped
1 tbsp chopped fresh oregano
2 tbsp butter
salt and pepper
4 fresh oregano sprigs, to garnish
freshly grated Parmesan cheese,
  to serve

1 Bring a large pan of lightly salted water to a boil over a medium heat. Add the pasta and cook for 8–10 minutes, or until done.

2 Bring a pan of salted water to a boil over a medium heat. Add the broccoli and cook. Avoid overcooking, so it retains its color and texture.

3 Heat the mascarpone and blue cheeses together in a large pan over a low heat until melted. Stir in the chopped oregano and season to taste. with salt and pepper.

4 Drain the pasta thoroughly and return to the pan. Add the butter and toss the pasta until coated thoroughly. Drain the broccoli well and add to the pasta with the sauce, tossing gently to mix.

5 Transfer the pasta to 4 large, warmed serving plates and garnish with fresh oregano sprigs. Serve with Parmesan cheese.

fettuccine all'alfredeo

serves four

2 tbsp butter

scant 1 cup heavy cream

1 lb/450 g fresh fettuccine

1 cup freshly grated Parmesan
    cheese, plus extra to serve

pinch of freshly grated nutmeg

salt and pepper

1 fresh Italian parsley sprig,
    to garnish

VARIATION

This classic Roman dish is often
served with the addition of ham
and peas. Add 2 cups shelled
cooked peas and 6 oz/175 g ham
strips with the cheese in step 4.

---

1 Put the butter and ⅔ cup of the cream in a large pan and bring the mixture to a boil over a medium heat. Reduce the heat, then simmer gently for about 1½ minutes, or until the cream has thickened slightly.

2 Meanwhile, bring a large pan of lightly salted water to a boil over a medium heat. Add the pasta and cook for about 2–3 minutes, or until done. Drain the pasta thoroughly and return to the pan, then pour over the cream sauce.

3 Toss the pasta in the sauce over a low heat until thoroughly coated.

4 Add the remaining cream, Parmesan cheese, and nutmeg to the pasta mixture, and season to taste with salt and pepper. Toss the pasta thoroughly in the mixture while gently heating through.

5 Transfer the pasta mixture to a large, warmed serving plate and garnish with a fresh parsley sprig. Serve immediately, handing extra grated Parmesan cheese separately.

pasta with pesto vinaigrette

serves six

2 cups dried pasta spirals

4 tomatoes, peeled

½ cup ripe black olives

2 tbsp sun-dried tomatoes in
   oil, drained

2 tbsp pine nuts, toasted

2 tbsp freshly grated Parmesan cheese

1 fresh basil sprig, to garnish

PESTO VINAIGRETTE

4 tbsp chopped fresh basil

1 garlic clove, minced

2 tbsp freshly grated
   Parmesan cheese

4 tbsp olive oil

2 tbsp lemon juice

salt and pepper

1 Bring a large pan of lightly salted water to a boil over a medium heat. Add the pasta and cook for 8–10 minutes, or until done. Drain the pasta thoroughly, rinse well in hot water, then drain again. Set aside.

2 To make the pesto vinaigrette, whisk the basil, garlic, Parmesan cheese, oil, and lemon juice together in a small bowl until well blended. Season with pepper to taste.

3 Put the pasta into a bowl, pour the pesto vinaigrette over it, and toss thoroughly.

4 Cut the tomatoes into wedges. Halve and pit the olives and slice the sun-dried tomatoes. Add the tomatoes, olives, and sun-dried tomatoes to the pasta and toss well.

5 Transfer the pasta to a salad bowl and sprinkle the pine nuts and Parmesan cheese over the top. Garnish with a basil sprig and serve warm.

pasta provencale

serves four

2 cups dried penne

1 tbsp olive oil

2 tbsp pitted ripe black olives,
drained and chopped

2 tbsp dry-pack sun-dried tomatoes,
soaked, drained, and chopped

14 oz/400 g canned artichoke
hearts, drained and halved

4 oz/115 g baby zucchini, trimmed
and sliced

4 oz/115 g baby plum
tomatoes, halved

3½ oz/100 g assorted baby
salad greens

salt and pepper

shredded basil leaves, to garnish

DRESSING

4 tbsp strained tomatoes

2 tbsp low-fat unsweetened yogurt

1 tbsp unsweetened orange juice

1 small bunch fresh basil, shredded

1 Bring a large pan of lightly salted water to a boil over a medium heat. Add the pasta and cook until done. Drain the pasta thoroughly and return to the pan. Stir in the oil, salt and pepper, olives, and sun-dried tomatoes, then let cool.

2 Gently mix the artichokes, zucchini, and plum tomatoes into the cooked pasta. Arrange the salad leaves in a serving bowl.

VARIATION

For a non-vegetarian version, stir 225 g/8 oz canned tuna in brine, drained and flaked, into the pasta together with the vegetables. Other pasta shapes can be included – look out for farfalle (bows) and rotelle (spoked wheels).

3 To make the dressing, mix all the ingredients together and toss into the vegetables and pasta.

4 Spoon the mixture on top of the salad and garnish with basil.

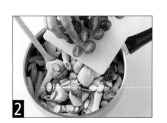

spaghetti bolognese

serves four

1 tbsp olive oil

1 onion, chopped finely

2 garlic cloves, chopped

1 carrot, chopped

1 celery stalk, chopped

¼ cup pancetta or lean bacon, diced

1½ cups lean ground beef

14 oz/400 g canned
   chopped tomatoes

2 tsp dried oregano

scant ½ cup red wine

2 tbsp tomato paste

salt and pepper

1 lb 7 oz/650 g fresh spaghetti or
   12 oz/350 g dried spaghetti

VARIATION

Try adding ¼ cup dried porcini,
soaked for 20 minutes in
2 tbsp of warm water,
to the bolognese sauce in
step 4, if you wish.

---

1 Heat the oil in a large skillet over a high heat. Add the onions and cook for 3 minutes.

2 Add the garlic, carrot, celery, and pancetta or bacon, and cook for about 3–4 minutes, or until just starting to brown.

3 Add the beef and cook over a high heat for 3 minutes, or until the meat has browned.

4 Stir in the tomatoes, oregano, and red wine and bring to a boil over a high heat. Reduce the heat and simmer for about 45 minutes.

5 Stir in the tomato paste and season with salt and pepper.

6 Bring a pan of lightly salted water to a boil over a medium heat. Add the pasta and cook for about 8–10 minutes, or until done. Drain.

7 Transfer the pasta to 4 serving plates and pour over the sauce. Toss to mix well and serve with Parmesan cheese, if you wish.

pasticcio

serves four

2 cups dried fusilli

4 tbsp heavy cream

1 tbsp olive oil for brushing

salt

fresh rosemary sprigs, to garnish

mixed salad greens, to serve

SAUCE

2 tbsp olive oil

1 onion, sliced thinly

1 red bell pepper, seeded
    and chopped

2 garlic cloves, chopped

5¼ cups ground beef

14 oz/400 g canned
    chopped tomatoes

½ cup dry white wine

2 tbsp chopped fresh parsley

2 oz/55 g canned anchovy fillets,
    drained and chopped

salt and pepper

TOPPING

1¼ cups unsweetened plain yogurt

3 eggs

pinch of freshly grated nutmeg

½ cup freshly grated
    Parmesan cheese

1 Heat the oil in a skillet over a medium heat. Add the onion and red pepper and cook for 3 minutes. Add the garlic and cook for 1 minute. Add the beef and cook until browned.

2 Add the tomatoes and wine and bring to a boil over a medium heat. Reduce the heat and simmer for 20 minutes, or until thickened. Stir in the parsley and anchovies, and season to taste with salt and pepper.

3 Bring a large pan of lightly salted water to a boil over a medium heat. Add the pasta and cook until almost done. Drain and transfer to a bowl. Stir in the cream.

4 For the topping, beat the yogurt, eggs, and nutmeg together.

5 Brush an ovenproof dish with oil. Spoon in half the pasta and cover with half the meat sauce. Repeat, then spread over the topping and sprinkle with the grated Parmesan cheese.

6 Bake in a preheated oven at 375°F/190°C, for 25 minutes, or until golden. Garnish with a rosemary sprig and serve with salad greens.

meatballs in italian red wine sauce

serves four

⅔ cup milk

2 cups white bread crumbs

12 shallots, chopped

4 cups ground steak

1 tsp paprika

1 lb/450 g dried egg tagliarini

salt and pepper

fresh basil sprigs, to garnish

ITALIAN RED WINE SAUCE

2 tbsp butter

8 tbsp olive oil

3 cups sliced exotic mushrooms

¼ cup whole-wheat flour

⅞ cup beef bouillon

⅔ cup red wine

4 tomatoes, peeled and chopped

1 tbsp tomato paste

1 tsp brown sugar

1 tbsp finely chopped fresh basil

1 Put the bread crumbs into a bowl and pour over the milk. Let soak for 30 minutes.

2 Heat half the butter and half the oil in a pan over a low heat. Add the mushrooms and fry for 4 minutes. Stir in the flour and cook for 2 minutes. Add the bouillon and wine and cook for 15 minutes. Add the tomatoes, tomato paste, sugar, and basil. Season to taste with salt and pepper and cook for 30 minutes.

3 Mix the shallots, steak, and paprika with the bread crumbs and season. Shape into 16 meatballs.

4 Heat the remaining oil and the remaining butter in a skillet. Add the meatballs, and fry until browned. Transfer to a casserole dish, pour over sauce, cover and cook in a preheated oven, at 350°F/180°C, for 30 minutes.

5 Bring a large pan of lightly salted water to a boil over a medium heat. Add the pasta and cook for 8–10 minutes, or until done. Drain and transfer to a serving dish. Remove the casserole from the oven and pour the meatballs and sauce onto the pasta. Garnish with a basil sprig and serve.

tagliatelle with pumpkin & prosciutto

serves four

1 lb 2 oz/500 g pumpkin or
butternut squash, peeled

2 tbsp olive oil

1 onion, chopped finely

2 garlic cloves, minced

4–6 tbsp chopped fresh parsley

pinch of freshly grated nutmeg

1¼ cups chicken or
vegetable bouillon

4 oz/115 g prosciutto

9 oz/250 g dried tagliatelle

⅝ cup heavy cream

salt and pepper

freshly grated Parmesan cheese,
to serve

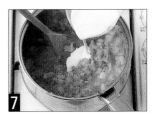

1 Cut the pumpkin or butternut squash in half and scoop out the seeds with a spoon. Cut the pumpkin or squash into ½-inch/1-cm dice.

2 Heat the oil in a large pan over a low heat. Add the onion and garlic and cook for about 3 minutes, or until softened. Add half the parsley and cook for 1 minute.

3 Add the pumpkin pieces and cook for 2–3 minutes. Season to taste with salt, pepper, and nutmeg.

4 Add half the bouillon to the pan and bring to a boil over a medium heat. Cover and simmer for about 10 minutes, or until the pumpkin is tender. Add more bouillon if the pumpkin is becoming dry and looks as if it might burn.

5 Add the prosciutto to the pan and cook, stirring frequently, for an additional 2 minutes.

6 Meanwhile, bring a large pan of lightly salted water to a boil over a medium heat. Add the pasta and cook for 12 minutes, or until done. Drain the pasta thoroughly and transfer to a large, warmed serving dish.

7 Stir the cream into the pumpkin and ham mixture and heat through. Spoon over the pasta, then sprinkle over the remaining parsley. Serve with the grated Parmesan cheese separately.

rare beef pasta salad

serves four

1 lb/450 g rump or sirloin steak in
   1 piece
1⅓ cups dried fusilli
4 tbsp olive oil
2 tbsp lime juice
2 tbsp Thai fish sauce
   (see Cook's Tip)
2 tsp honey
4 scallions, sliced
1 cucumber, peeled and cut into
   1-inch/2.5-cm chunks
3 tomatoes, cut into wedges
3 tsp finely chopped fresh mint
salt and pepper

COOK'S TIP

Thai fish sauce, also known
as nam pla, is made from salted
anchovies. It has a strong flavor,
so should be used with care.

1   Season the steak with salt and
pepper. Broil or pan-fry the steak
for about 4 minutes on each side. Let
stand for 5 minutes, then slice thinly
across the grain.

2   Meanwhile, bring a large pan of
lightly salted water to a boil over
a medium heat. Add the pasta and
cook until done. Drain the pasta
thoroughly, then refresh in cold water
and drain again. Return the pasta to
the pan and toss in the oil.

3   Mix the lime juice, fish sauce, and
honey together in a small pan
and cook over a medium heat for
about 2 minutes.

4   Add the scallions, cucumber,
tomatoes, and chopped mint to
the pan, then add the steak and mix
well. Season with salt to taste.

5   Transfer the pasta to a large,
warmed serving dish and top
with the steak mixture. Serve just
warm or let cool completely.

spicy sausage salad

serves four

1 cup small dried pasta shapes,
   such as elbow tubetti

2 tbsp olive oil

1 medium onion, chopped

2 garlic cloves, minced

1 small yellow bell pepper, seeded
   and cut into very thin sticks

6 oz/175 g spicy pork sausage, such
   as chorizo, Italian pepperoni or
   salami, skinned and sliced

2 tbsp red wine

1 tbsp red wine vinegar

mixed salad greens, chilled

salt

2 Heat the oil in a pan over a
   medium heat. Add the onion and
cook until translucent, stir in the garlic,
yellow bell pepper, and sliced sausage,
and cook for 3–4 minutes, stirring once
or twice.

3 Add the wine, wine vinegar, and
   reserved pasta to the pan, stir to
blend well, and bring the mixture just
to a boil over a medium heat.

4 Arrange the chilled salad greens
   onto 4 serving plates, spoon on
the warm sausage and pasta mixture,
and serve immediately.

VARIATION

Other suitable sausages include
the Italian pepperoni, flavored
with chili peppers, fennel, and
spices, and one of the many
varieties of salami, usually
flavored with garlic and pepper.

---

1 Bring a large pan of lightly salted
   water to a boil over a medium
heat. Add the pasta and cook until
done. Drain and set aside.

pasta with chicken sauce

serves four

9 oz/250 g fresh green tagliatelle

1 tbsp olive oil

salt and pepper

fresh basil leaves, to garnish

TOMATO SAUCE

2 tbsp olive oil

1 small onion, chopped

1 garlic clove, chopped

14 oz/400 g canned
    chopped tomatoes

2 tbsp chopped fresh parsley

1 tsp dried oregano

2 bay leaves

2 tbsp tomato paste

1 tsp sugar

CHICKEN SAUCE

4 tbsp unsalted butter

14 oz/400 g boned chicken breasts,
    skinned and cut into thin strips

¾ cup blanched almonds

1¼ cups heavy cream

salt and pepper

1 To make the tomato sauce, heat the oil in a pan over a medium heat. Add the onion and cook until translucent. Add the garlic and cook for 1 minute. Stir in the tomatoes, parsley, oregano, bay leaves, tomato paste, and sugar. Season to taste with salt and pepper, bring to a boil and simmer, uncovered, for 15–20 minutes, or until reduced by half. Remove the pan from the heat and discard the bay leaves.

2 To make the chicken sauce, melt the butter in a skillet over a medium heat. Add the chicken and almonds and cook for 5–6 minutes, or until the chicken is cooked through.

3 Meanwhile, bring the cream to a boil in a small pan over a low heat and boil for about 10 minutes, or until reduced by almost half. Pour the cream over the chicken and almonds, stir and season to taste with salt and pepper. Set aside and keep warm.

4 Bring a large pan of lightly salted water to a boil over a medium heat. Add the pasta and oil and cook for 8–10 minutes, or until done. Drain the pasta and transfer to a warmed serving dish. Spoon over the tomato sauce and arrange the chicken sauce down the center. Garnish with the basil leaves and serve immediately.

stuffed cannelloni

serves four

8 dried cannelloni tubes

⅓ cup freshly grated
Parmesan cheese

fresh herb sprigs, to garnish

FILLING

2 tbsp butter

1½ cups frozen spinach, thawed,
drained, and chopped

½ cup ricotta cheese

⅓ cup freshly grated
Parmesan cheese

¼ cup chopped ham

pinch of freshly grated nutmeg

2 tbsp heavy cream

2 eggs, beaten lightly

salt and pepper

BÉCHAMEL SAUCE

2 tbsp butter

scant ¼ cup all-purpose flour

1¼ cups milk

2 bay leaves

pinch of freshly grated nutmeg

1 To make the filling, melt the butter in a pan over a low heat. Add the spinach and cook for 2–3 minutes. Remove from the heat and stir in the ricotta and Parmesan cheeses, and the ham. Season with nutmeg, salt, and pepper. Beat in the cream and eggs to make a thick paste.

2 Bring a large pan of lightly salted water to a boil over a medium heat. Add the pasta and cook for 10–12 minutes, or until done. Drain the pasta thoroughly and let cool.

3 To make the sauce, melt the butter in a pan over a low heat. Stir in the flour and cook, stirring, for 1 minute. Gradually whisk in the milk. Add the bay leaves and simmer, whisking gently for 5 minutes. Add the nutmeg, salt and pepper. Remove from the heat and discard the bay leaves.

4 Spoon the filling into a pastry bag and use to fill the cannelloni.

5 Spoon a little sauce into the bottom of an ovenproof dish. Put the cannelloni in a single layer on the sauce, then pour over the remaining sauce. Sprinkle the Parmesan cheese over and cook in a preheated oven at 375°F/190°C, for 40–45 minutes. Garnish with fresh herb sprigs and serve immediately.

neapolitan veal chops with mascarpone

serves four

⅞ cup butter

4 x 9 oz/250 g veal chops, trimmed

1 large onion, sliced

2 apples, peeled, cored, and sliced

6 oz/175 g white mushrooms

1 tbsp chopped fresh tarragon

8 black peppercorns

1 tbsp sesame seeds

14 oz/400 g dried marille

scant ½ cup extra virgin olive oil

¾ cup mascarpone cheese, broken
    into small pieces

2 large beefsteak tomatoes, cut
    in half

leaves of 1 fresh basil sprig

salt and pepper

1 Melt 4 tablespoons of the butter in a skillet over a low heat. Cook the veal for 5 minutes on each side. Transfer to a dish and keep warm.

2 Put the onion and apples into the skillet and cook until lightly browned. Transfer to a dish, then put the veal on top and keep warm.

3 Melt the remaining butter in the skillet over a low heat. Add the mushrooms, tarragon, and peppercorns and cook for 3 minutes. Sprinkle over the sesame seeds.

4 Bring a large pan of lightly salted water to a boil over a medium heat. Add the pasta and cook for about 8–10 minutes, or until done. Drain the pasta thoroughly and transfer to a large ovenproof casserole dish

5 Top the pasta with the mascarpone and sprinkle over the oil. Put the onions, apples, and veal chops on top of the pasta. Spoon the mushrooms and peppercorns onto the chops, then arrange the tomatoes and

basil leaves around the edge and season to taste with salt and pepper. Cook in a preheated oven at 300°F/150°C, for about 5 minutes.

6 Remove from the oven and transfer to 4 serving plates. Serve.

chicken tortellini

serves four

4 oz/115 g boned chicken
   breast, skinned

2 oz/55 g prosciutto

2 tbsp cooked spinach, well drained

1 tbsp finely chopped onion

2 tbsp freshly grated Parmesan cheese

pinch of ground allspice

1 egg, beaten

1 lb/450 g Homemade Pasta Dough
   (see page 6)

all-purpose flour, for dusting

salt and pepper

2 tbsp chopped fresh parsley,
   to garnish

SAUCE

1 cup light cream

2 garlic cloves, minced

⅔ cup white mushrooms,
   sliced thinly

4 tbsp freshly grated
   Parmesan cheese

1 Bring a pan of salted water to a boil over a medium heat. Add the chicken and cook for 10 minutes. Let cool slightly, then put into a blender, with the prosciutto, spinach, and onion and process until finely chopped. Stir in 2 tablespoons of the Parmesan cheese, the allspice, and beaten egg, and season to taste with salt and pepper.

2 Roll out the pasta dough thinly on a lightly floured counter and cut into 1½–2-inch/4–5-cm circles.

3 Put ½ tsp of the filling in the center of each circle. Fold the

pieces in half and press the edges to seal. Wrap each piece around your finger, cross over the ends and curl the rest of the dough backward to make a navel shape. Re-roll the trimmings and repeat until all the dough is used up.

4 Bring a large pan of lightly salted water to a boil over a medium heat. Add the tortellini, in batches, and cook for 5 minutes. Drain thoroughly and transfer to a serving dish.

5 To make the sauce, put the cream and garlic into a small pan and bring to a boil over a low heat, then simmer for 3 minutes. Add the mushrooms and half the Parmesan cheese, season and simmer for 2–3 minutes. Pour the sauce over the tortellini, sprinkle over the remaining Parmesan cheese, garnish with the chopped parsley and serve.

pasta & pork in cream sauce

serves four

1 lb/450 g pork tenderloin,
   sliced thinly

4 tbsp olive oil

225 g/8 oz white mushrooms, sliced

⅞ cup Italian Red Wine Sauce
   (see page 38)

1 tbsp lemon juice

pinch of saffron

3 cups dried orecchioni

4 tbsp heavy cream

12 quail eggs (see Cook's Tip)

salt

COOK'S TIP

In this recipe, the quail eggs are
soft-cooked. As they are
extremely difficult to shell when
warm, it is important that they
are thoroughly cooled first.
Otherwise, they will break up
unattractively.

1 Put the pork slices between 2 sheets of plastic wrap and pound until wafer thin, then cut into strips.

2 Heat the oil in a large skillet over a medium heat. Add the pork slices and cook for 5 minutes. Add the mushrooms and cook for an additional 2 minutes.

3 Pour over the Italian Red Wine Sauce (see page 38), reduce the heat and simmer gently for 20 minutes.

4 Meanwhile, bring a large pan of lightly salted water to a boil over a medium heat. Add the lemon juice, saffron, and pasta and cook for about 8–10 minutes, or until done. Drain the pasta thoroughly and keep warm.

5 Stir the cream into the pan with the pork and heat gently for a few minutes.

6 Boil the eggs for 3 minutes in a small pan of boiling water. Cool in cold water and remove the shells.

7 Transfer the pasta to a large, warmed serving plate, top with the pork and the sauce, and garnish with the eggs. Serve immediately.

lasagna verde

serves four

1 tbsp butter for greasing

14 sheets precooked lasagna

generous 3 cups Béchamel Sauce
(see page 44)

1⅓ cups freshly grated
mozzarella cheese

1 fresh basil sprig, to garnish

MEAT SAUCE

2 tbsp olive oil

2 cups ground beef

1 large onion, chopped

1 celery stalk, diced

4 garlic cloves, minced

¼ cup all-purpose flour

½ pint beef bouillon

¼ pint red wine

1 tbsp chopped fresh parsley

1 tsp chopped fresh marjoram

1 tsp chopped fresh basil

2 tbsp tomato paste

salt and pepper

1 To make the meat sauce, heat
the oil in a large skillet over a
medium heat. Add the ground beef
and cook, stirring frequently, until
browned. Add the onion, celery, and
garlic and cook for 3 minutes.

2 Sprinkle over the flour and cook,
stirring, for 1 minute. Gradually
stir in the bouillon and wine. Season
with salt and pepper and add the
herbs. Bring to a boil, reduce the heat
and simmer for 35 minutes. Add the
tomato paste and cook for 10 minutes.

3 Lightly grease an ovenproof dish
with the butter. Arrange sheets of
lasagna over the bottom of the dish,
spoon over a layer of meat sauce, then
Béchamel Sauce (see page 44). Repeat
the process twice, finishing with a layer
of Béchamel Sauce. Sprinkle over the
mozzarella cheese.

4 Cook the lasagna in a preheated
oven at 375°F/190°C, for
35 minutes, or until the top is golden
brown and bubbling. Garnish with a
basil sprig and serve immediately
straight from the dish.

chicken & spinach lasagna

serves four

2 cups frozen chopped spinach,
    thawed, and drained

½ tsp ground nutmeg

1 lb/450 g lean, cooked chicken
    meat, skinned and diced

4 sheets precooked lasagna verde

1½ tbsp cornstarch

1¾ cups skim milk

scant ¾ cup freshly grated
    Parmesan cheese

salt and pepper

TOMATO SAUCE

14 oz/400 g canned
    chopped tomatoes

1 onion, chopped finely

1 garlic clove, minced

⅔ cup white wine

3 tbsp tomato paste

1 tsp dried oregano

1 To make the tomato sauce, put the tomatoes into a pan and stir in the onion, garlic, wine, tomato paste, and oregano. Bring to a boil over a low heat and simmer gently for 20 minutes until thick. Season well.

2 Drain the spinach again and spread it out on paper towels to make sure that as much water as possible is removed. Layer the spinach in the bottom of a large ovenproof dish, then sprinkle with ground nutmeg and season to taste with salt and pepper.

3 Arrange the diced chicken over the spinach and spoon over the tomato sauce. Arrange the sheets of lasagna over the tomato sauce.

4 Blend the cornstarch with a little of the milk to make a smooth paste. Pour the remaining milk into a pan and stir in the paste. Heat gently for 2–3 minutes, stirring, until the sauce thickens. Season well.

5 Spoon the sauce over the lasagna and transfer the dish to a cookie sheet. Sprinkle the grated cheese over the sauce and cook in a preheated oven at 400°F/200°C, for 25 minutes, or until golden, then serve.

51

lemon chicken conchiglie

serves four

8 chicken pieces (about
    4 oz/115 g each)

4 tbsp butter, melted

4 tbsp mild mustard (see Cook's Tip)

2 tbsp lemon juice

1 tbsp brown sugar

1 tsp paprika

3 tbsp poppy seeds

3½ cups fresh pasta shells

1 tbsp olive oil

salt and pepper

COOK'S TIP

Dijon is the type of mustard most
often used in cooking, as it has a
clean and only mildly spicy flavor.
German mustard has a sweet-
sour taste, with Bavarian
mustard being slightly sweeter.
American mustard is mild
and sweet.

1 Arrange the chicken pieces,
smooth-side down, in a single
layer in a large ovenproof dish.

2 Mix the butter, mustard, lemon
juice, sugar, and paprika together
in a bowl and season to taste with salt
and pepper. Brush the mixture over the
upper surfaces of the chicken pieces
and cook in a preheated oven at
400°F/200°C, for 15 minutes.

3 Remove the dish from the oven
and, using tongs, carefully turn
over the chicken pieces. Coat the upper
surfaces of the chicken with the
remaining mustard mixture, then
sprinkle with poppy seeds. Return to
the oven for an additional 15 minutes.

4 Meanwhile, bring a large pan of
lightly salted water to a boil over a
medium heat. Add the pasta shells and
oil and cook until done.

5 Drain the pasta and arrange in a
large, warmed serving dish. Top
with the chicken, pour over the sauce
and serve immediately.

corsican clam spaghetti

serves four

14 oz/400 g dried spaghetti

salt and pepper

CORSICAN CLAM SAUCE

2 lb/900 g live clams

4 tbsp olive oil

3 large garlic cloves, minced

pinch of chili flakes (optional)

2 lb/900 g tomatoes, peeled and
    chopped, with juice set aside

½ cup pitted green or ripe black
    olives, chopped

1 tbsp chopped fresh oregano or
    ½ tsp dried oregano

1 To make the sauce, put the clams into a bowl of lightly salted water and let soak for 30 minutes. Rinse them under cold running water and scrub lightly to remove any sand from the shells.

2 Discard any broken clams or open clams that refuse to close when firmly tapped. This indicates they are dead and can cause food poisoning if eaten. Put the clams soak into a large bowl of water and let soak. Meanwhile, bring a large pan of lightly salted water to a boil over a medium heat.

3 Heat the oil in a large skillet over a medium heat. Add the garlic and chili flakes (if using), and cook, stirring constantly, for about 2 minutes.

4 Stir in the tomatoes, olives, and oregano. Reduce the heat and simmer, stirring frequently, until the tomatoes soften and start to break up. Cover and simmer for 10 minutes.

5 Meanwhile, add the pasta to the pan of boiling water, bring back to a boil, and cook for 8–10 minutes, or until done. Drain the pasta

thoroughly, and set aside about ½ cup of the cooking liquid. Return the pasta to the pan and keep warm.

6 Add the clams and reserved cooking liquid to the sauce and stir. Bring to a boil over a medium heat, stirring constantly. Discard any clams that have not opened and transfer the sauce to a larger pan.

7 Add the pasta to the sauce and toss until well coated, then transfer the pasta to 4 large, warmed serving dishes. Serve immediately.

spaghetti al tonno

serves four

7 oz/200 g canned tuna, drained

2 oz/55 g canned anchovy
   fillets, drained

1 cup olive oil

1 cup coarsely chopped
   Italian parsley

⅔ cup sour cream

1 lb/450 g dried spaghetti

2 tbsp butter

salt and pepper

ripe black olives, to garnish

1 Remove any bones from the tuna, then put the tuna, anchovies, oil, and parsley into a food processor or blender and process until a smooth sauce is formed.

2 Spoon the sour cream into the food processor or blender and process again for a few seconds to blend thoroughly. Season to taste with salt and pepper.

3 Bring a large pan of lightly salted water to a boil over a medium heat. Add the pasta and cook for about 12 minutes, or until done.

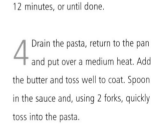

4 Drain the pasta, return to the pan and put over a medium heat. Add the butter and toss well to coat. Spoon in the sauce and, using 2 forks, quickly toss into the pasta.

5 Remove the pan from the heat and transfer the pasta to 4 large, warmed serving plates. Garnish with the olives and serve immediately.

squid & macaroni stew

serves four

2 cups dried short-cut macaroni or
    other small pasta shapes

6 tbsp olive oil

2 onions, sliced

12 oz/350 g prepared squid, cut
    into 1½-inch/4-cm strips

1 cup fish bouillon

⅝ cup red wine

12 oz/350 g tomatoes, peeled and
    sliced thinly

2 tbsp tomato paste

1 tsp dried oregano

2 bay leaves

2 tbsp chopped fresh parsley

salt and pepper

1 Bring a large pan of lightly salted water to a boil over a medium heat. Add the macaroni and cook for 3 minutes. Drain, then return to the pan. Cover and keep warm.

2 Heat the oil in a pan over a medium heat. Add the onions and cook until translucent. Add the squid and bouillon and simmer for 5 minutes. Pour in the wine and add the tomatoes, tomato paste, oregano, and bay leaves. Bring to a boil, then season to taste with salt and pepper and cook for 5 minutes.

3 Stir the macaroni into the pan, then cover and simmer for about 10 minutes, or until the squid and

macaroni are tender and the sauce has thickened. If the sauce remains too liquid, uncover the pan and continue cooking for a few minutes.

4 Remove the bay leaves and discard. Set aside a little parsley and stir the remainder into the pan. Transfer to a large, warmed serving dish and sprinkle over the remaining parsley. Serve immediately.

red mullet fillets with orecchiette

serves four

3¾ cups all-purpose flour

8 red mullet fillets

2 tbsp butter

⅝ cup fish bouillon

1 tbsp crushed almonds

1 tsp pink peppercorns

1 orange, peeled and cut
    into segments

1 tbsp orange liqueur

grated peel of 1 orange

1 lb/450 g dried orecchiette

1 tbsp olive oil

⅝ cup heavy cream

4 tbsp amaretto

salt and pepper

TO GARNISH

2 tbsp snipped fresh chives

1 tbsp toasted almonds

1 Season the flour with salt and pepper and sprinkle into a shallow bowl. Press the fish fillets into the flour to coat. Melt the butter in a skillet over a low heat. Add the fish and cook for about 3 minutes, or until browned.

2 Add the fish bouillon to the skillet and cook for 4 minutes. Carefully transfer the fish to a heatproof plate, cover with foil and keep warm.

3 Add the almonds, pink peppercorns, half the orange, the orange liqueur, and orange peel to the skillet. Simmer until the liquid has reduced by half.

4 Meanwhile, bring a large pan of lightly salted water to a boil over a medium heat. Add the pasta and cook for 15 minutes, or until done.

5 Meanwhile, season the sauce with salt and pepper and stir in the cream and amaretto. Cook for 2 minutes. Return the fish fillets to the skillet to coat with the sauce.

6 Drain the pasta and transfer to a serving dish. Top with the fish fillets and the sauce. Garnish with the remaining orange segments, chives, and toasted almonds. Serve.

poached salmon with penne

serves four

4 x 10 oz/275 g fresh salmon steaks

2½ tbsp butter

¾ cup dry white wine

pinch of sea salt

8 peppercorns

1 fresh dill sprig

1 fresh tarragon sprig

1 lemon, sliced

4 cups dried penne

2 tbsp olive oil

¼ cup all-purpose flour

⅔ cup warm milk

juice and finely grated peel of
    2 lemons

2 oz/55 g arugula, chopped

salt and pepper

TO GARNISH

lemon slices

arugula

1 Put the salmon into a large, non-stick skillet. Add 2 tablespoons of the butter, wine, sea salt, peppercorns, dill, tarragon, and lemon slices. Bring to a boil over a medium heat, cover and simmer for 10 minutes.

2 Using a spatula, carefully remove the salmon. Strain and set aside the cooking liquid. Remove and discard the salmon skin and center bones, then put into a warmed dish, cover and keep warm.

3 Meanwhile, bring a large pan of lightly salted water to a boil over a medium heat. Add the pasta and cook for 12 minutes, or until done. Drain and sprinkle with the remaining oil. Put into a warmed serving dish, top with the salmon and keep warm.

4 Melt the remaining butter in a pan over a low heat and stir in the flour for 2 minutes. Stir in the milk and 7 tablespoons of the cooking liquid. Add the lemon juice and peel and cook for an additional 10 minutes.

5 Add the arugula to the sauce, stir gently and season to taste with salt and pepper.

6 Pour the sauce over the salmon, garnish with lemon slices and arugula. Serve immediately.

spaghetti & shellfish

serves four

2 cups dried spaghetti, broken into
15-cm/6-inch lengths

2 tbsp olive oil

1¼ cups chicken bouillon

1 tsp lemon juice

1 small cauliflower, cut
into flowerets

2 carrots, sliced thinly

4 oz/115 g snow peas

4 tbsp butter

1 onion, sliced

8 oz/225 g zucchini, sliced

1 garlic clove, chopped

12 oz/350 g frozen, cooked, shelled
shrimp, thawed

2 tbsp chopped fresh parsley

¼ cup freshly grated
Parmesan cheese

½ tsp paprika

salt and pepper

4 unshelled, cooked shrimp,
to garnish

crusty bread, to serve

1 Bring a pan of lightly salted water
to a boil over a medium heat.
Add the pasta and and cook until
done. Drain the pasta thoroughly and
return to the pan. Toss with the oil,
cover and keep warm.

2 Bring the chicken bouillon and
lemon juice to a boil over a
medium heat. Add the cauliflower and
carrots and cook for 3–4 minutes.
Remove from the pan and set aside.
Add the snow peas to the pan and
cook for 1–2 minutes. Set aside with
the other vegetables.

3 Melt half the butter in a large
skillet over a medium heat. Add
the onion and zucchini and cook for
about 3 minutes. Add the garlic and
shrimp and cook for an additional
2–3 minutes, or until heated through.

4 Stir in the reserved vegetables
and heat through. Season to taste
with salt and pepper and stir in the
remaining butter.

5 Transfer the pasta to a warmed
serving dish. Pour over the sauce
and add the parsley. Toss well until
coated. Sprinkle over the Parmesan
cheese and paprika and garnish with
the shrimp. Serve with crusty bread.

pasta & chili tomatoes

serves four

10 oz/280 g dried pappardelle

3 tbsp groundnut oil

2 garlic cloves, minced

2 shallots, sliced

8 oz/225 g green beans, sliced

3½ oz/100 g cherry
   tomatoes, halved

1 tsp chili flakes

4 tbsp crunchy peanut butter

⅔ cup coconut milk

1 tbsp tomato paste

VARIATION

Add slices of chicken or beef to
the recipe and stir-fry with the
beans and pasta in step 3 for a
more substantial main meal.

---

1 Bring a large pan of lightly salted water to a boil over a medium heat. Add the pasta and cook for about 8–10 minutes, or until done. Drain the pasta thoroughly and set aside.

2 Meanwhile, heat a large wok over a high heat. Add the oil and when hot, add the garlic and shallots. Cook for 1 minute.

3 Add the green beans and drained pasta to the wok, and cook for about 5 minutes. Add the cherry tomatoes and mix well.

4 Mix the chili flakes, peanut butter, coconut milk, and tomato paste together. Pour the chili mixture into the wok, toss well and heat through.

5 Transfer the pasta to 4 large, warmed serving dishes and serve immediately.

vegetable ravioli

serves four

1 lb/450 g Homemade Pasta Dough
   made without tarragon
   (see page 6)
6 tbsp butter
⅔ cup light cream
¾ cup freshly grated
   Parmesan cheese
fresh basil sprigs, to garnish
FILLING
2 large eggplants
3 large zucchini
6 large tomatoes
1 large green bell pepper
1 large red bell pepper
3 garlic cloves
1 large onion
½ cup olive oil
2 tbsp tomato paste
½ tsp chopped fresh basil
salt and pepper

1 To make the filling, cut the eggplants and zucchini into 1-inch/2.5-cm chunks. Put the eggplant pieces into a strainer, sprinkle liberally with salt and set aside for 20 minutes. Rinse and drain, then pat dry on paper towels.

2 Blanch the tomatoes in boiling water for 2 minutes. Drain, peel, and chop the flesh. Core and seed the peppers and cut into 1-inch/2.5-cm dice. Chop the garlic and onion.

3 Heat the oil in a pan over a low heat. Add the garlic and onion and cook, stirring occasionally, for about 3 minutes.

4 Stir in the eggplants, zucchini, tomatoes, bell peppers, tomato paste, and basil. Season to taste with salt and pepper, cover and simmer for 20 minutes, stirring frequently.

5 Roll out the Pasta Dough (see page 6) and cut out 3-inch/7.5-cm circles with a plain cutter. Put a spoonful of the vegetable filling on each circle. Dampen the edges slightly and fold the pasta circles over, pressing together to seal.

6 Bring a pan of lightly salted water to a boil over a medium heat. Add the ravioli and cook for about 3–4 minutes. Drain and transfer to an ovenproof dish, dotting each layer with butter. Pour over the cream and sprinkle over Parmesan cheese. Cook in a preheated oven at 400°F/200°C, for 20 minutes. Garnish with a basil sprig and serve immediately.

summertime tagliatelle

serves four

1 lb 7 oz/650 g zucchini

6 tbsp olive oil

3 garlic cloves, minced

3 tbsp chopped fresh basil

2 fresh red chilies, seeded and sliced

juice of 1 large lemon

5 tbsp light cream

4 tbsp freshly grated
   Parmesan cheese

8 oz/225 g dried tagliatelle

salt and pepper

COOK'S TIP

Lime juice could be used instead
of the lemon. As limes are
usually smaller, squeeze the juice
from 2 fruits.

1 Using a swivel vegetable
peeler, slice the zucchini into
thin ribbons.

2 Heat the oil in a skillet over a low
heat. Add the garlic and cook for
30 seconds.

3 Add the zucchini ribbons and
cook, stirring constantly, for
3–5 minutes. Stir in the basil, chilies,
lemon juice, cream, and Parmesan
cheese and season to taste with salt
and pepper. Keep warm.

4 Meanwhile, bring a large pan of
lightly salted water to a boil over
a medium heat. Add the pasta and
cook for 8–10 minutes, or until done.
Drain the pasta thoroughly and transfer
to a large, warmed serving bowl.

5 Pile the zucchini mixture on top of
the pasta and serve immediately.

chili & red bell pepper pasta

serves four

2 red bell peppers, halved
   and seeded

1 small fresh red chili

2 garlic cloves

4 tomatoes, halved

1¾ oz/50 g ground almonds

7 tbsp olive oil

1 lb 8 oz/675 g fresh pasta or
   12 oz/350 g dried pasta

fresh oregano leaves, to garnish

1 Put the bell peppers, skin-side up, onto a cookie sheet with the chili, garlic, and tomatoes. Cook under a preheated hot broiler for 15 minutes, or until charred. After 10 minutes, turn the tomatoes skin-side down.

2 Put the bell peppers and chili into a plastic bag and let them sweat for 10 minutes.

3 Using a sharp knife, remove the skin from the bell peppers and chili and slice the flesh into strips.

4 Peel the garlic and peel and seed the tomatoes.

5 Put the almonds onto a cookie sheet and cook under the broiler for 2–3 minutes, or until golden.

VARIATION

Add 2 tbsp of red wine vinegar to the sauce and use as a dressing for a cold pasta salad, if you prefer.

6 Put the bell peppers, chili, garlic, and tomatoes into a food processor or blender and blend to a paste. Keep the motor running and slowly add the oil to form a thick sauce. Alternatively, put the mixture into a bowl and mash with a fork. Beat in the oil, drop by drop.

7 Stir the toasted ground almonds into the mixture.

8 Put the sauce into a pan and warm until it is heated through.

9 Bring a large pan of lightly salted water to a boil over a medium heat. Add the pasta and cook for about 8–10 minutes, or until done. Drain the pasta thoroughly and transfer to 4 large, warmed serving dishes. Pour over the sauce and toss to mix. Garnish with fresh oregano leaves and serve.

pasta with nuts & cheese

serves four

1 cup pine nuts

3 cups dried pasta shapes

1¼ cups broccoli flowerets

2 zucchini, sliced

1 cup full-fat soft cheese

⅔ cup milk

1 tbsp chopped fresh basil

4½ oz/125 g white
    mushrooms, sliced

3 oz/85 g blue cheese, crumbled

salt and pepper

fresh basil sprigs, to garnish

salad greens, to serve

1 Sprinkle the pine nuts onto a cookie sheet and cook under a preheated broiler, turning occasionally, until lightly browned. Set aside.

2 Bring a large pan of lightly salted water to a boil over a medium heat. Add the pasta and cook for about 8–10 minutes, or until done.

3 Bring a large pan of lightly salted water to a boil over a medium heat. Add the broccoli and zucchini and cook for 5 minutes.

4 Put the soft cheese into a pan and heat over a low heat, stirring. Stir in the milk. Add the basil and mushrooms, and cook for 2–3 minutes. Stir in the blue cheese and season to taste with salt and pepper.

5 Drain the pasta and vegetables, and mix together. Pour the cheese and mushroom sauce over, and add the pine nuts. Toss gently to mix them in. Transfer to 4 serving dishes and garnish with basil sprig. Serve with salad greens.

paglia e fieno

serves four

4 tbsp butter

1 lb/450 g fresh peas, shelled

⅞ cup heavy cream

1 lb/450 g mixed fresh green and
white spaghetti or tagliatelle

⅔ cup freshly grated
Parmesan cheese

pinch of freshly grated nutmeg

salt and pepper

fresh Parmesan cheese shavings,
to serve

VARIATION

Cook 2 cups sliced white or
exotic mushrooms in 4 tbsp of
butter over a low heat for
4–5 minutes. Stir into the peas
and cream sauce just before
adding to the pasta in step 4.

---

1 Melt the butter in a large pan over a low heat. Add the peas and cook for 2–3 minutes.

2 Using a measuring cup, pour ⅝ cup of the cream into the pan. Bring to a boil over a low heat and simmer for 1–1½ minutes, or until slightly thickened. Remove the pan from the heat.

3 Meanwhile, bring a large pan of lightly salted water to a boil over a medium heat. Add the pasta and cook for 2–3 minutes, or until done. Remove the pan from the heat and drain the pasta thoroughly, then return to the pan.

4 Add the peas and cream sauce to the pasta. Return the pan to the heat, then add the remaining cream and the Parmesan cheese and season to taste with salt, pepper, and freshly grated nutmeg.

5 Using 2 forks, gently toss the pasta to coat with the peas and cream sauce, while heating through.

6 Transfer the pasta to 4 warmed serving dish and serve with shavings of Parmesan cheese.

spaghetti & mushroom sauce

serves four

4 tbsp butter

1 tbsp olive oil

6 shallots, sliced

6 cups sliced white mushrooms

1 tsp all-purpose flour

⅝ cup heavy cream

2 tbsp port

½ cup sun-dried tomatoes, chopped

freshly grated nutmeg

1 lb/450 g dried spaghetti

1 tbsp chopped fresh parsley

salt and pepper

1 fresh parsley sprig, to garnish

6 triangles of fried white bread,
   to serve

1 Heat the butter and the oil in a pan over a medium heat. Add the shallots and cook for 3 minutes. Reduce the heat, add the mushrooms and cook for 2 minutes. Season and sprinkle over the flour. Cook, stirring, for 1 minute.

2 Gradually stir in the cream and port, then add the sun-dried tomatoes and a pinch of grated nutmeg, and cook over a low heat for 8 minutes.

3 Meanwhile, bring a large pan of lightly salted water to a boil over a medium heat. Add the pasta and cook for 12–14 minutes, or until done.

VARIATION

Non-vegetarians could add 4 oz/115 g prosciutto, cut into thin strips and heated gently in 2 tbsp butter, to the pasta with the mushroom sauce.

4 Drain the pasta and return to the pan. Pour over the mushroom sauce and cook for 3 minutes. Transfer the pasta to a large serving plate, sprinkle over the chopped parsley. Garnish with a parsley sprig and serve with crispy triangles of fried bread.

penne & vegetables

serves four

2 cups dried penne

2 tbsp olive oil

2 tbsp butter

2 garlic cloves, minced

1 green bell pepper, seeded and
   sliced thinly

1 yellow bell pepper, seeded and
   sliced thinly

16 cherry tomatoes, halved

1 tbsp chopped oregano

½ cup dry white wine

2 tbsp pitted ripe black olives, cut
   into fourths

2¾ oz/75 g arugula

salt and pepper

fresh oregano sprigs, to garnish

VARIATION

If arugula is unavailable, spinach
makes a good substitute. Follow
the same cooking instructions
as for arugula.

---

1 Bring a pan of lightly salted water
to a boil over a medium heat.
Add the pasta and cook for about
8–10 minutes, or until done. Drain the
pasta thoroughly.

2 Heat the oil and butter in a pan
over a low heat. Add the garlic
and cook for 30 seconds. Add the bell
peppers and cook, stirring occasionally,
for 3–4 minutes.

3 Stir in the tomatoes, oregano,
wine, and olives and cook for
3–4 minutes. Season and stir in the
arugula until just wilted.

4 Transfer to a serving dish, spoon
over the sauce and garnish with
an oregano sprig. Serve.

This is a Parragon Publishing Book
This edition published in 2004

Parragon Publishing
Queen Street House
4 Queen Street
Bath BA1 1HE, UK

ISBN: 1-40543-622-0

Printed in China

NOTE

Cup measurements in this book are for American cups. This book also uses
imperial and metric measurements. Follow the same units
of measurement throughout; do not mix imperial and metric.
All spoon measurements are level: teaspoons are assumed to be 5 ml and
tablespoons are assumed to be 15 ml. Unless otherwise stated, milk is assumed
to be whole milk, eggs and individual vegetables such as potatoes are medium,
and pepper is freshly ground black pepper.

The times given for each recipe are an approximate guide only because the
preparation times may differ according to the techniques used by different
people and the cooking times may vary as a result of the type of oven used.

Recipes using raw or very lightly cooked eggs should be
avoided by infants, the elderly, pregnant women, convalescents, and anyone
suffering from an illness.